The

Virginia Company
of London

❧

1606-1624

Wesley Frank Craven

CLEARFIELD

Originally published
1957

Reprinted for
Clearfield Company, Inc. by
Genealogical Publishing Co., Inc.
Baltimore, Maryland
1993, 1995, 1997, 2004

International Standard Book Number: 0-8063-4555-1

Made in the United States of America

*Jamestown 350th Anniversary Historical Booklet
Number 5*

THE VIRGINIA COMPANY OF LONDON, 1606-1624

This is the story of the Virginia Company and only indirectly of the Virginia colony. Those who seek an account of the early years at Jamestown should turn to another number in this same series. Here the focus belongs to the adventurers in England whose hopes gave shape to the settlement at Jamestown, and whose determination brought the colony through the many disappointments of its first years. In terms of time, the story is short, for it begins with the granting of the first Virginia charter in 1606 and ends with the dissolution of the company in 1624. It thus covers a period of only eighteen years, but during these years England's interest in North America was so largely expressed through the agency of the Virginia Company that its story constitutes one of the more significant chapters in the history both of the United States and of the British Empire.

In the beginning there were two companies of the Virginia adventurers, the one having its headquarters in London and the other in the western outport of Plymouth. Englishmen at that time used the name Virginia to designate the full sweep of the North American coast that lay above Spanish Florida. In the original Virginia charter the adventurers were granted rights of exploration, trade, and settlement on the "Coast of Virginia or America" within limits that reached from 34° of latitude in the south to 45° in the north, which is to say from the mouth of the Cape Fear River in lower North Carolina to a point midway through the modern state of Maine. The Plymouth grantees had a primary interest in the northern area that Captain John Smith would later name New England, and there they established a colony at Sagadahoc in August 1607, only a few weeks after the settlement of Jamestown. But the colony barely survived the winter, and was abandoned in the spring of 1608. Thereafter, the Plymouth adventurers gave up. In contrast, the London adventurers persisted, and their persistence served to tie the name of Virginia increasingly to them and to their more southerly settlement. As a result, the London adventurers became in common usage the Virginia adventurers, their company the Virginia Company, and their colony Virginia.

The Virginia colony was especially fortunate in having the backing of London. Indeed, it may not be too much to suggest that the chief difference between the stories of Roanoke Island and of Jamestown was the difference that London made. Consistently, the leadership of Elizabethan adventures to North America, including those of Gilbert and Raleigh, had come from the western counties and outports of England, and with equal consistency hopeful projects had foundered on the inadequacy of their financial support while London favored other ventures—to Muscovy, to the Levant, and more recently to the East Indies. It was not merely that London had the necessary capital and credit for a sustained effort; it also had experience in the management of large and distant ventures, such as those of the East India Company over which Sir Thomas Smith presided, as he would preside through many years over the Virginia Company. London had too the advantage of its proximity to the seat of government in nearby Westminster, where King James had his residence, where the highest courts of the realm sat periodically, and where England's parliament customarily met. Already, in 1606, it was possible to trace in the immediate environs of the ancient City of London, itself still medieval in appearance and in the organization of much of its life, the broad outlines of the great metropolis that has been increasingly the focal point of England's development as a modern state.

In thus emphasizing the importance of London to the early history of Virginia, one runs the risk of misrepresenting the true character of the Virginia adventure. Contrary to the impression that will be gained from many of our modern textbooks, the Virginia Company represented much more than the commercial interests of the port of London. Its membership included many gentlemen and noblemen of consequence in the kingdom. Some of them, no doubt, became subscribers to a Virginia joint-stock for the same reason that often led members of the landed classes in England into commercial ventures. But others, quite evidently, subscribed because of a sense of public responsibility, or simply because skilfully managed propaganda had put pressure on them to accept a responsibility of social or political position. For the Virginia adventure was a public undertaking, its aim to advance the fortunes of England no less than the fortunes of the adventurers themselves.

It would be helpful if we knew more about the original Virginia adventurers than we do. The records are so incomplete as to make impossible anything approaching a full list of the first subscribers. However, enough is known to suggest the broad range of experience and interest belonging to those who now joined in a common effort to build an empire for England in America. The original charter of 1606 lists only eight of the adventurers by name, they being the ones in whose names the petition for the charter had been made. This list omits Sir John Popham, Lord Chief Justice of the Kings Bench, who may well have been the prime mover in the enterprise, and Sir Thomas Smith, who was an active leader from an early date. Four of the eight men listed are identified as belonging to the London group. Sir Thomas Gates was a soldier and veteran of campaigns in the Netherlands who would later serve as the colony's governor. Sir George Somers had led many attacks against Spanish possessions in Queen Elizabeth's day, was a member of parliament, and would meet his death four years later in Bermuda while on a mission of rescue for Virginia. Edward Maria Wingfield was another soldier who had fought in the Netherlands. He belonged to a family which had acquired extensive estates in Ireland, and he too would go to Virginia, where he served as first president of the colony's council. The most interesting of the four was Richard Hakluyt, a clergyman whose chief mission in life had been the encouragement of overseas adventures by his fellow countrymen. To them he had literally given a national tradition of adventure by compiling and editing one of the more influential books in England's history—*The Principall Navigations, Voyages, and Discoveries of the English Nation*, whose reading, in Michael Drayton's words, inflamed "Men to seeke fame." Hakluyt had been advisor to both Gilbert and Raleigh in their ventures, and since then he had consistently promoted the idea that England might best find in North America the opportunities that were needed for her prosperity and her security.

A significant indication of the extent to which the public interest was considered to be involved in the Virginia project is found in the provision that was first made for the government of the two colonies. The powers of government, which is to say the ultimate right to decide and to direct, were vested in a royal council, commonly known as the Virginia Council and having its seat in London. Its membership was probably drawn exclusively from the two groups of Virginia adventurers, but the members were appointed by the king and were sworn to his special service. Among the first members were Sir Thomas Smith, chief of the London merchants; Sir William Wade, lieutenant of the London Tower; Sir Walter Cope, member of parliament for Westminster and adventurer in a variety of overseas enterprises; Sir Henry Montague, recorder of the City of London; Solicitor General John Doderidge, subsequently justice of the Kings Bench; Sir Ferdinando Gorges, who later would lead a reviving interest in the settlement of New England and still later would become an enemy of the Puritans who so largely accomplished that task; Sir Francis Popham, son and heir to the Lord Chief Justice; and John Eldred of London, Thomas James of Bristol, and James Bagge of Plymouth, each of these three being described as a merchant. This assignment of the powers of government proved to be awkward, and it denied the adventurers direct control over the more important questions affecting their adventures, as in the choice of a plan of government for the colony or in the appointment of its key officers. Consequently, the adventurers secured a change in the second Virginia charter, granted in 1609. It was then specified that members of the council thereafter should be "nominated, chosen, continued, displaced, changed, altered and supplied, as death, or other several occasions shall require, out of the Company of the said Adventurers, by the voice of the greater part of the said Company and Adventurers, in their Assembly for that purpose." In language less repetitious than that used by the company's lawyer, this meant that the council now became an agent primarily of the adventurers. Even so, the king retained a veto over any choice they might make, for members of the council were still required to take a special oath administered by one of the high officers of state, and refusal to give the oath could mean disqualification for the office. The company's later history would show, whatever its legal advisor may have assumed in 1609, that this requirement was no mere formality.

It is not easy for the modern American to read with full assurance the scanty record of Virginia's first years. How, for example, should he interpret the suggestion at the beginning of the first charter that the adventurers sought chiefly to propagate the "Christian Religion to such people, as yet live in darkness and miserable ignorance of the true knowledge and worship of God?" It is simple enough to point out that the first adventurers in Jamestown showed very little of the missionary's spirit, that they included only one minister, and that he had enough to do in ministering to the English settlers. It is also easy to draw an obvious contrast between the dedicated missionaries who so frequently formed the vanguard of Spanish and French settlement in America and the adventurous and often unruly men who first settled Virginia. In the absence of immediate and continuing missionary endeavors, one is naturally inclined to dismiss professions of a purpose to convert the Indian as nothing more than a necessary gesture toward convention in an age that was still much closer to the medieval period than to our own. And yet, on second thought, one begins to wonder just how sophisticated such a conclusion may be. He remembers how deep was the rift between Protestantism and Catholicism at that time, how fundamental to the patriotism of an Englishman was his long defense of a Protestant church settlement against the threat of Catholic Spain, and how largely the issues of religious life still claimed the first thoughts of men. He then may feel inclined to observe that the English adventurers, after all, did undertake to establish a mission in Virginia at a relatively early date. True, ten years elapsed before the effort to provide a school and college for the Indians had its beginning, but these were years of a continuing struggle for the very life of the colony itself. In the circumstances, perhaps ten years should be viewed as a short time.

Be that as it may, there are other questions that have been even more bothersome, if only because they have seemed more pertinent to the modern interest in Virginia's history. The American has been accustomed to view the Virginia colony as the first permanent settlement in his country, as the point at which his own history has its beginning, but he finds in the Jamestown colony a pattern of activity somewhat different from that he associates with the later development of the country. What kind of a colony was it? Was it really a colony? Just what were the adventurers trying to accomplish in Virginia? Were they actually interested in colonization, in the proper sense of the term, or were their objectives commercial? These and other such questions have claimed much of the attention of those who have sought to interpret for their fellow countrymen the early history of Virginia. The difficulty arises partly from the American's insistence that the later history of his country be taken as the standard for judging every action of the first adventurers, and partly from a failure to appreciate the extent to which the earlier ventures in Virginia were necessarily exploratory in character.

If one of us could ask the adventurers in 1606 what it was they hoped to accomplish in America, he probably would be told that it depended very much on what they might find there. Although Richard Hakluyt had been most industrious in collecting available information from the earlier explorations of North America, including those by Spanish and French explorers, the specific information at hand was quite definitely limited. By the close of the sixteenth century European explorers had charted the broad outlines of the North American coast, and here and there they had filled in much of the detail, as had the French in Canada, the Spaniard and the Frenchman on the coast of Florida, and the Englishman along the coastal regions to be later known as Carolina and New England. But the information at the command of the adventurers in one country was not always available to those of another; indeed, within any one country there were shipmasters who carried in their heads working charts of coastal waters wholly unknown to the geographers and cartographers who sought to serve the larger interests of the nation. Thus the London adventurers in 1606, though having at hand a substantial body of useful information regarding the coasts, the winds, and the currents running northward from the West Indies past St. Augustine to Cape Hatteras, and comparable information regarding the more northern waters explored by Frobisher, Davis, Gilbert, and others, had only a sketchy knowledge of the intervening coastline that would soon be explored by Captain Samuel Argall on commission from the Virginia Company and by Henry Hudson, an Englishman temporarily in the service of Dutch merchants. Even Chesapeake Bay, to which the London adventurers dispatched their first expedition, was known to them chiefly by the reports of Indians interrogated by Raleigh's agents as they worked out from Roanoke Island. The first colonists in Virginia gave to London detailed information regarding the lower Chesapeake and the James River, but not until 1608 did Captain John Smith find the time to explore the upper reaches of the bay and to identify the great rivers emptying into it there. It hardly seems necessary to argue the utility of such explorations, to which eloquent testimony exists in the new bounds immediately fixed for the colony in the second charter. But many have been the attempts to pass judgment on the success or failure of the first settlers at Jamestown that have been written as though their primary assignment had not been to explore.

Exploration and fortification—these two terms are consistently linked in the papers on which the early English adventurers jotted notes for their guidance or for the instruction of their agents in America. The very first objective of the explorers was to locate a suitable site for fortification, in order that further explorations might be conducted from a secure base. The fortifications to be raised had to meet exacting standards, such as would be approved by the military engineers with whom the adventurers consulted along with the geographers, the cartographers, and the shipmasters who also possessed useful information. For these fortifications were intended to provide security not so much against the native Indian as against the ships and soldiers of Spain. Over the years there had been some debate as to how the fort might be best located, with the result that in 1607 it was decided to locate it some distance up a river that would afford navigation for an ocean-going vessel but would force the enemy to fight his way inland against the disadvantage of the warning that could be given by an outer guard at the mouth of the river. Such were the considerations that shaped the choice of Jamestown as the site of the first permanent English settlement in North America. To stand in the middle of the Jamestown peninsula for contemplation of its many disadvantages for the purposes of agricultural settlement, and even for the health of its people, is to lose sight of the main point. One should walk over against the river, and consider there the field of fire that was open for well placed guns.

And just what was the Jamestown fort supposed to guard? Was it the few acres of the modern county of James City, or the right of Englishmen to possess the Virginia peninsula, where so much of importance to our national history has found its place? Not at all. It was the right of Englishmen to be in North America, to fish the waters that lay off its coast, to trade with its inhabitants, and to exploit such other opportunities as an unexplored and undeveloped continent might offer. How far these opportunities might lead no one could tell in advance—perhaps even to China.

A trade with China had been a major objective of English adventure since the middle of the sixteenth century, when the Muscovy Company had had its origins in an attempt to find a northeast passage around the Scandinavian peninsula leading to Cathay—Marco Polo's fabulous kingdom of northern China. The explorers found instead a profitable trade with the territories of Ivan the Terrible, but the Muscovy merchants continued to support a variety of ventures seeking the establishment of an Oriental trade. Their agents looked into the possibilities of an overland trade through Russia to Cathay, and experimented none too profitably with a trans-Russia trade with Persia. They gave their support to renewed attempts to find a northeast passage and claimed a right of license for the numerous efforts that were made in Elizabeth's reign to find a northwest passage around or through North America. Failing in these efforts, the English merchants finally had challenged Portugal's monopoly of trade with the East Indies by way of the Cape of Good Hope. The East India Company, chartered by Elizabeth in 1600, had gotten off to a good start, and was destined to become one of the great empire builders of Britain's history. In 1606, however, the East India merchants had had just enough experience with the new trade to begin to appreciate some of its difficulties, as in the need

9

to employ larger and more expensive ships than were standard in England's maritime trade and the great distance to China by way of the Cape of Good Hope. Perhaps, after all, some route through America might have the advantage over the Cape route. In the opinion of the late Sir William Foster, through many years historiographer of the India Office, this was a chief reason for the interest Sir Thomas Smith took in Virginia.

Let it be noted that Sir Thomas' interest in Virginia outlasted the hope that a successful search for a passage to China might be based on Jamestown. Nevertheless, the point may help to explain the marked emphasis on this hope that one finds at the beginning of the project. Instructions to the first expedition directed the choice of a seat on some navigable river, and added, "if you happen to discover divers portable rivers, and mongst them any one that hath two main branches, if the difference be not great make choice of that which bendeth most toward the North-West, for that way you shall soonest find the other sea." The other sea, of course, was the Pacific, or as Englishmen were likely to say, the South Seas, whose waters also washed the shores of China. Vain as was this hope of trade with the Orient through America, it was destined for survival, in one form or another, through many years. As late as the middle of the nineteenth century, it would be a principal argument for the construction of a trans-continental railway.

In 1606 the supposition was that the river system of North America might be like that of Russia, where easy portages joining rivers flowing in different directions made it possible to travel, most of the way by boat, from the north to the south of the country and return. "You must observe," advised the adventurers, "whether the river on which you plant doth spring out of mountains or out of lakes; if it be out of any lake, the passage to the other sea will be the more easy, and [it] is like enough that out of the same lake you shall find some spring which runs the contrary way toward the East India Sea; for the great and famous rivers of Volga, Tanis and Dwina have three heads near joynd, and yet the one falleth into the Caspian Sea, the other into the Euxine Sea, and the third into the Polonian Sea." For this information, the Virginia adventurers were indebted to the Muscovy Company, with which Captain Christopher Newport, who commanded the ships dispatched to Virginia, had formerly served. It was a good enough working theory, based partly on knowledge of the geography of Russia and partly on interrogation of the Indians in Carolina by Raleigh's men. And the rivers of that part of North America which lies east of the Mississippi form just such a system as the Virginia adventurers envisaged, except for the fact that the Ohio and other westward flowing streams do not empty into the Pacific.

The modern American has usually looked upon such a venture as this as something distinctly apart from an agricultural type of endeavor, but there is good reason for believing that the London adventurers took a different view. They understood the dependence of agriculture upon an opportunity to market its products, and they considered the success of their commercial ventures to be the surest and the quickest way of providing easy access to a market. If a new and practicable route to China could be found in America, any colony located close at hand to the portage along which the goods of the Orient were moved for transshipment to England would find a ready market for food and other provisions by supplying the ships engaged in a highly profitable trade. More than that, the plenty and the regularity of this shipping would provide easy freightage for the encouragement of a variety of agricultural and horticultural experiments looking to the production of such commodities as sugar, ginger, wine, or vegetable dyes and oils. The adventurers well understood the advantage to be gained by duplicating the success previously won by the Portuguese and Spaniards with such experiments in the Azores, in Madeira, in the Canaries, and more recently in the West Indies.

11

To put the point briefly, Virginia was founded upon many different hopes for profitable undertakings—some of them commercial, some agricultural, and some industrial. The records show an early interest in several extractive industries, including mining, not just for gold but for copper and iron as well. First instructions for trade with the native Indians reveal an immediate concern for the establishment of good relations with them and for laying in a good stock of Indian corn as a food reserve, but they show too a concern for the policies that would shape the development of a wider trade. Provision in the charter, and in the instructions of the royal council, for the creation of individual estates according to the laws and customs of England, not to mention the guarantee of full legal rights for the inhabitants of the colony and for their children, leave no more room for speculation as to the intended permanence of the settlement than there is doubt as to the expected diversity of its economic activity. But for the time being, first things must take first place. Until it had been demonstrated that Virginia could provide profitable freightage for the ships of England, her future rested upon an insecure foundation. Hence, the initial emphasis on the type of activity which promised the more immediate or the greater return.

Newport's fleet of the *Susan Constant*, the *Godspeed*, and the *Discovery* sailed for Virginia in December 1606. While the adventurers waited for his return and report on the first discoveries, the Spanish ambassador excitedly reported to Spain that the English intended to send two vessels to Virginia each month until "they have 2,000 men in that country." Actually the plan seems to have been quite different. Lord Chancellor Egerton is reported to have declared in 1609: "We . . . thought at first we would send people there little by little." Whatever the plan, this was the practice. Newport's total complement in the first fleet was 160 men of whom 104 remained in the colony. He was back at Plymouth by late July 1607, and from Plymouth he came on to London in August. For cargo he carried clapboard, and his sailors had picked up so much sassafras root that the leaders of the colony feared that the market for this established staple of the American trade might be ruined. He brought with him also ore which he hoped an assay would prove to be gold, and he declared the country to be rich in copper. With some exaggeration, he announced explorations "into the country near two hundred miles" and the discovery of "a river navigable for great shippes one hundred and fifty miles." The adventurers responded by sending him out again, in October 1607, with 120 prospective settlers and what would be greeted in Jamestown as the first supply.

All told, Captain Newport would make five round trips between England and Virginia before ending a career that included service of the Muscovy Company by dying on the island of Java as an agent of the East India Company. He has found no important place in the American tradition, partly because Captain John Smith, the Virginia colony's first historian, took care to see that Captain Newport did not have a hero's role. But those of us who would understand the context in which our history first developed will do well to consider the career of Christopher Newport.

In carrying out the second supply, which reached Jamestown in September 1608, Newport had aboard 70 new colonists, including two women and eight Polish and German experts in the manufacture of glass, tar, pitch, and soap ashes. He had a broad commission for completing the exploration of the James River above the falls that much later would fix the site of Richmond, and for determining the fate of Raleigh's lost colony. He found no answer to that riddle, which remains to our own day an intriguing mystery; indeed, he seems not to have found the time for any real investigation of the problem. As a result, he brought back only rumors of four survivors living on the Chowan River. The instruction gains its chief interest from the suggestion it conveys of a renewed interest on the part of the adventurers in the area previously explored by Raleigh's men. Perhaps the adventurers anticipated the further disappointments resulting from the additional exploration of the James, and so thought again of the Roanoke River, which Captain Ralph Lane had partly explored in 1585 and 1586 with the hope that it might lead to China. Perhaps they had an eye mainly for the publicity that could be had for any news of Raleigh's colonists. Whatever the fact, a renewed interest in the Carolina region would find very concrete expression in a new charter the adventurers secured shortly after Newport's return to England in January 1609.

The actual bounds of the Jamestown colony under the first Virginia charter ran 100 miles along the coast and 100 miles inland from the coast. This, at any rate, was the area to which title was promised by the charter. The second charter gave title to an area reaching 200 miles both northward and southward along the coast from Point Comfort, at the mouth of the James, and "up into the Land throughout from Sea to Sea, West and Northwest." In these greatly enlarged bounds one immediately detects three major interests: (1) a desire to control the entire extent of any passage that might be found to the South Seas, (2) the hope that something might be accomplished in Carolina, and (3) the need for a title to the whole of the Chesapeake, whose exploration had been completed by Captain John Smith in the preceding summer. In this exploration Captain Smith had pointed the way for the colony's later expansion, but at the moment the adventurers seem to have viewed the Chesapeake as having value chiefly for its fish and trade and for further exploration. Dissatisfied with Jamestown, as a place that was both unhealthy and exposed to attack from the sea, they advised Sir Thomas Gates, on the eve of his departure for Virginia in the spring of 1609 as the newly appointed lieutenant governor of the colony, to move his principal city above the falls on the James, where he would enjoy every advantage in an attack by a European foe, or better still, that he locate it on the Chowan River in modern

North Carolina, "foure dayes Journey from your forte Southe-wards." In an earlier passage of his instructions, he had already been advised that he should be guided by the general principle of seeking the sun, "which is under God the first cause both of health and Riches."

Those who bother to read Gates' instructions will notice the emphasis they place on the choice of a *principal* seat. There were to be other towns, and Jamestown would be kept as the chief port of entry, though not as the site of the main magazine and storehouse. All told, perhaps three "habitations" would be enough for the settlers now to be transported. Their number was nothing less than 600 persons, men, women, and children —more than all the men who had been sent to Virginia in the preceding two years. If the reported statement of Lord Chancellor Egerton be accepted, the adventurers after two years of explora-tory effort had come to feel that "the proper thing is to fortify ourselves all at once, because when they will open their eyes in Spain they will not be able to help it, and even tho' they may hear it, they are just now so poor that they will have no means to prevent us from carrying out our plan." It was indeed a poor year for Spain, which in 1609 had to agree to a truce in the long struggle with the Dutch that ultimately brought legal rec-ognition of the independence of Holland. This was the year which also witnessed the exploration by Henry Hudson of the river that has ever since borne his name, a river on which the Dutch would soon lay the foundations of a shortlived North American empire. Only the year before had the French built their fort at Quebec. And now the English were determined to fortify Virginia "all at once." A once proud monopoly of the new world, and of its opportunities, was to be finally broken.

The London to which Newport returned late in January, 1609, was already astir with preparations for an adventure such as England had never seen before. He sat in consultation with Sir Thomas Smith, as did Richard Hakluyt, and Thomas Hariot,

15

who as a young man just out of Oxford had gone to Roanoke Island for Raleigh in 1585, and whose *True Report of Virginia*, published in 1588, still remained a chief dependence of the London adventurers. Hakluyt was preparing for publication a translation of the Gentleman of Elva's account of De Soto's expedition through the southeastern part of the later United States, an account published in April as *Virginia Richly Valued*. To this he added in June a translation from Marc Lescarbot's *Histoire de la Nouvelle-France* for the purpose of demonstrating that Virginia "must be far better by reason it stands more southerly nearer to the sun." Broadsides scattered about London announced the special opportunities awaiting those who would join in the new venture, while clergymen in their pulpits lent the aid of divine sanction, as in Robert Gray's *Good Speed to Virginia*. The broad outlines of the new plan had been presented to the public in February by Alderman Robert Johnson in a tract entitled *Nova Britannia: Offering Most Excellent Fruites by Planting in Virginia*. By the end of that month the adventurers had also completed negotiations for the granting of the second charter, and had opened their books for subscription to a new joint-stock fund.

The device of the joint-stock fund had been increasingly relied upon by English adventurers as they sought the means for financing more distant and more expensive ventures. It had the advantage of pooling the resources of more than one individual, and of distributing the risk, and the Virginia adventure had depended upon joint-stock methods of finance from the beginning. It is impossible to speak with exactness regarding the financial arrangements of the first years. A provision in the first instructions directing the settlers to live, work, and trade together in a common stock through a period of five years suggests the possibility of a five-year terminable stock, i.e., a fund that would be invested and reinvested through a term of five years before it was divided, together with the earnings thereon. But other evidence indicates that there may have been a separate stock for each of Newport's voyages, as was the case with each of the early voyages of the East India Company to the Orient. The so-called joint-stock company of that day rarely had a permanent joint-stock of the sort identified with the modern corporation. Instead, it functioned as a governing body representing all of the merchants engaged in a particular trade, who traded individually or through a variety of joint-stocks invested under the general regulation of the company. And such was the character of the Virginia Company.

Whatever may have been the specific terms offered earlier investors, those offered in 1609 are clear enough. It was proposed that men subscribe at the rate of £12 10s. per share to a common stock that would be invested and reinvested over the term of the next seven years. Although special good fortune might justify a dividend of some part of the earnings at an earlier date, there would be no final dividend, which at that time meant a division of capital as well as the earnings thereof, until 1616. The dividend promised then would include a grant of land in Virginia as well as a return of the capital with profit. How much land depended, like the profit, on the degree of success that had attended the venture meantime.

One of the inducements for subscription was a promise that all adventurers would have a voice in determining the policies of the company. Again, it is impossible to say just what had been the organization through which the adventurers had previously functioned. They probably followed custom by meeting in assemblies or courts (both terms were common) when some joint decision was needed, and no doubt they relied on the designation of such committees and officers as were necessary for the execution of decisions reached in their assembly. It may be that the adventurers sitting on the Virginia Council functioned also in the character of an executive committee for their fellows. In view of the well known tendency for institutions to evolve out of earlier practices, with such adjustments as experience may dictate, there is reason for believing that important features of the organization outlined in the second charter were older than the charter itself. But the charter of 1609 offers the first unmistakable evidence as to the organization upon which the adventurers depended.

They were there incorporated by the name of "The Treasurer and Company of Adventurers and Planters of the City of London, for the first Colony in Virginia." Sir Thomas Smith was designated treasurer with power to warn and summon the members of the council and of the company "to their courts and meetings." The adventurers, "or the major part of them which shall be present and assembled for that purpose" were empowered to make grants of land according to "the proportion of the adventurer, as to the special service, hazard, exploit, or merit of any person so to be recompenced, advanced, or rewarded." They were to meet also as occasion required for the election of members of the council, which was charged with the management of the enterprise on the ground that it was not convenient "that all the adventurers shall be so often drawn to meet and assemble." The members of the council were listed by name, more than fifty of them, beginning with Henry, Earl of Southampton, and including the Lord Mayor of London, the Lord Bishop of Bath and Wells, Thomas, Lord De la Warr, Sir William Wade, Sir Oliver Cromwell, Sir Francis Bacon, Sir Maurice Berkeley, Sir Thomas Gates, Sir Walter Cope, Sir Edwin Sandys, Sir Thomas Roe, Sir Dudley Digges, John Eldred, and John Wolstenholme. These and their colleagues of the council, which included of course Sir Thomas Smith, were the great men of the company, not necessarily the heaviest investors but those whose experience, or social and political position, argued that they should be on the managing board. In short, the subscribers had a basic right to choose the directors of the business

18

and to determine the division of its rewards, but the great men would run it.

For the assurance of the adventurers, each of them was listed by name in the charter—all told, some 650 of them. In addition to the individuals there named, the charter listed some fifty London companies which had subscribed in their corporate capacity in response to the appeals of London's clergymen and the Lord Mayor. To list all these companies would be tedious, but some of them should be named, if only for the picture they give of London itself. Here were "the Company of Mercers, the Company of Grocers, the Company of Drapers, the Company of Fishmongers, the Company of Goldsmiths, the Company of Skinners, the Company of Merchant-Taylors, the Company of Haberdashers, the Company of Salters, the Company of Ironmongers, the Company of Vintners, the Company of Clothworkers, the Company of Dyers, the Company of Brewers, the Company of Leathersellers, the Company of Pewterers, the Company of Cutlers," and others, including the companies to which belonged the city's cordwainers, barber-surgeons, masons, plumbers, innholders, cooks, coopers, bricklayers, fletchers, blacksmiths, joiners, weavers, plasterers, stationers, upholsterers, musicians, turners, and glaziers. This was a national effort, but in a special way it was London's effort to serve the nation in response to a call from its leaders.

There is reason to believe that the terms of the charter had been agreed upon by the end of February, but the document remained unsealed until May, when all who had subscribed could be listed. By that date, too, some 600 subjects of the king had agreed to make the adventure in person to Virginia. Some of them were smart enough to discount the propaganda that had persuaded them, and so they settled for the wages offered by the company. But others agreed to go on adventure, i.e. to accept the adventurers' offer that their personal adventure to Virginia would be counted as one share, at the minimum, in the common joint-stock. This was to say that they would be entitled to whatever rewards in 1616 might belong to any subscriber in England for £12 10s; and if the personal adventure of the settler in Virginia was considered to be worth more, as in the case of a surgeon or one of the high officers of the colony, then might the rights of an adventurer in Virginia run as high as any belonging to the great adventurers in England. The colonists who came to America in 1609 were thus encouraged to view themselves as being in no way inferior to those who sent them.

Sir George Somers had been selected as admiral of the great fleet which dropped down the Thames from London on May 15 and sailed from Plymouth on the second of June with a full complement of nine vessels. Somers rode aboard the *Sea Adventure*, whose master was Newport and whose passengers included Sir Thomas Gates and William Strachey, the newly appointed secretary of the colony. Ahead of them had gone Captain Samuel Argall, to find a new route to Virginia running north of the Spanish West Indies, and to make a test of the Chesapeake fisheries. Somers guided his ships along a route that had long been familiar to him, the route discovered by Columbus for Spain and the route that Newport and other English adventurers had consistently followed to the more southern parts of Virginia, but he tried to stay above the channels regularly followed by the ships of Spain. Such, at any rate, were his instructions, and for seven weeks out of Plymouth all went well. But then a storm struck, no doubt an early hurricane of the sort so familiar to residents of the east coast today, a storm which separated the *Sea Adventure* from the other vessels and carried it to destruction off the coast of Bermuda. Providence brought crew and passengers, all 150 of them, safely ashore to begin an idyll that would be celebrated in Shakespeare's *Tempest* and would be turned to advantage by the adventurers in their later propaganda. In Bermuda they found food in plenty—fish, fowl, and hogs that ran wild—and a most healthful climate. But for almost a year Virginia would struggle without the leadership of Somers, Newport, or Gates, and without the sure authority of instructions and commissions they had carried aboard the *Sea Adventure.*

After ten months the shipwrecked colonists had fashioned from the cedars of Bermuda, which reminded them of the cedars of Lebanon, two small vessels named the *Patience* and the *Deliverance.* The ships were stoutly enough built to carry the full company to Virginia in May 1610, but at Jamestown they found only want and confusion. The other vessels in Somers' fleet had straggled into the bay the preceding summer with their storm-tossed passengers, but the following winter had been a nightmare. This was the winter that was destined long to be remembered as the starving time, the time when one man was reported even to have eaten his wife. Only a handful of the settlers, new and old, had survived, and Somers and Gates saw no choice but to abandon the colony. It was saved by the providential arrival early in June of Lord De la Warr, who brought with him 150 new colonists and a commission as the colony's governor. Somers went back to Bermuda in the hope of laying in a stock of pork for Virginia, but there he died and his seamen ran for England.

The disturbing news of these tragic events reached London piecemeal. First came the news in the fall of 1609 that the *Sea Adventure,* with Somers, Gates, Newport, and Strachey, had been lost. This was a severe blow to the leaders of the company, who had planned to send De la Warr out with perhaps as many colonists as Somers had carried. Already the enthusiasm engendered by the promotional campaign of the preceding spring had begun to decline, as some men took second thought. Subscriptions at that time had been enlisted on an understanding that they might be paid in installments, and the adventurers now often found it difficult to collect what had been promised. During the winter they published an extraordinarily frank promotional piece, *A True and Sincere Declaration of the Purpose and Ends of the*

Plantation Begun in Virginia. In this pamphlet, they did the best they could to stir again the high hopes of the preceding spring, but they had to admit what all London knew, that the news was not encouraging. And so they appealed to the honor of the subscribers, that they remember those in Virginia who had staked their lives on the promises made by other men. It must be said that the adventurers did very well indeed, in the circumstances, to get De la Warr away in the spring with three vessels and 150 recruits for the colony.

Had he been able to send back a favorable report on the situation in Virginia, the adventurers probably would have found their position not too difficult. Instead, Sir Thomas Gates returned to London in September 1610 with a report that caused the adventurers to consider seriously whether the whole project should not be abandoned. Gates himself was subsequently credited with having clinched the decision in favor of continuance by arguing that sugar, wine, silk, iron, sturgeon, furs, timber, rice, aniseed, and other valuable commodities could be produced in Virginia, given the necessary time and support. The adventurers saw also the promotional possibilities of Somers' shipwreck at Bermuda, or rather, the remarkable experience which had followed it. Was this not an encouraging sign of God's providential care? Of His willingness to support the English in Virginia? This was a question London was invited to contemplate again and again during the months that followed.

No doubt, the courage of a few key leaders, among whom Sir Thomas Smith was now quite definitely the chief, had a large part in the decision to continue. Certainly, it took courage to launch the new campaign for funds to which the adventurers committed themselves in the fall of 1610. The estimated need ran to £30,000. All former subscribers were urged to subscribe another £37 10s. on agreement that the subscription would be paid in at the rate of £12 10s. per year over the next three years. Others were invited to subscribe on the same terms. The Lord

Mayor appealed once more to the London companies, and plans were made for inviting the other towns of England to contribute. In November the Company published *A True Declaration of the Estate of the Colonie in Virginia* for the purpose of refuting "scandalous reports" tending to discourage subscriptions. Richard Rich presented, probably at the suggestion of the adventurers, his *Newes from Virginia, the Lost Flocke Triumphant,* a poem celebrating the shipwreck of the *Sea Adventure* and the providential survival of its passengers. And to this Silvanus Jourdan added his *Discovery of the Barmudas,* a pamphlet recounting the experience of Somers and his colleagues in the islands. It was written, declared the author, "for the love of my country; and . . . the good of the plantation in Virginia."

It is not so remarkable that the adventurers failed to achieve their goal of £30,000 as that they actually secured the subscription of approximately £18,000 by the spring of 1611. The records of the company are so incomplete for any time prior to 1619, when the only surviving court minutes have their beginning, that it is impossible to give the comparative figures one would like to have. But there is evidence suggesting that the fund raised in 1609 may not have been larger than £10,000. If this be true, the success of this second campaign for funds becomes all the more remarkable. One can hardly explain it in terms of the ordinary calculations of a business community. Perhaps the adventurers believed their own propaganda, were themselves responsive to the kind of patriotic appeal that was made in the spring of 1610, when they were trying to get Lord De la Warr's expedition ready. "The eyes of all Europe," said the adventurers, "are looking upon our endeavours to spread the Gospell among the heathen people of Virginia, to plant an English nation there, and to settle a trade in those parts, which may be peculiar to our nation, to the end we may thereby be secured from being eaten out of all profits of trade by our more industrious neighbors."

With the new funds, the adventurers equipped two expeditions which sailed for Virginia in the spring of 1611. The first to leave carried 300 men, in three ships, under the command of Sir Thomas Dale, another veteran of the Netherlands fighting who had been commissioned as marshal of the colony. It was impossible not to be impressed by the evidence that a lack of discipline had contributed to the colony's woes, and Dale, who sailed in March, undoubtedly was intended to draw upon his experience as a soldier for the better discipline of the colonists. Sir Thomas Gates, who followed Dale out in May, had a broader task. He would continue to serve as the lieutenant governor under Lord De la Warr, and, like Dale, he carried 300 passengers. But his six ships also carried much more. One of the basic problems of original colonization, though it has often been lost sight of, was to stock the colony with cattle, hogs, poultry, etc. Later colonists, in Maryland or Carolina, would buy these essentials in Virginia, but the Virginia colonists had no established neighbor of their own nation on which to rely, and during the starving time they had literally eaten themselves out of stock. Nothing could better illustrate the fact that the Virginia adventurers in 1611 had to begin all over again than the 100 cattle, the 200 swine, and the poultry in unspecified numbers Gates had aboard his ships as they set their course westward. And if any one wishes to estimate the value of a cow that had been transported across the Atlantic, let him notice the penalty imposed by Dale's laws, so called, for killing one.

As Gates dropped down the Thames in May, the adventurers must have relaxed with the satisfaction that comes from real achievement. Twice now, within the span of two years, they had raised a great fund with which they sent each time nine vessels and 600 colonists to Virginia. Indeed, they had done even more. Counting Argall's ship, which sailed ahead of Somers in the spring of 1609, and the three vessels going over with De la Warr in 1610, the company had dispatched to Virginia no less than 22 vessels and close to 1,400 colonists in a two year period. But

Gates had hardly cleared the coasts of England before Lord De la Warr, of all persons, turned up in London, to the great consternation of his fellow adventurers.

A general assembly of the adventurers on June 25 listened to his explanation, which was promptly published by order of the council. The story briefly was this. Ever since he had reached Virginia the preceding June he had suffered a succession of violent sicknesses—fevers, the flux, gout, and finally scurvy, "till I was upon the point to leave the world." In preference to this he left Virginia in a vessel commanded by Argall, and in the hope that he might recover his health with the aid of hot baths in the West Indies. Contrary winds had forced him to alter his course to the Azores, where oranges and lemons had cured him of the scurvy. He then resolved to return to his post, but was persuaded to seek first a full recovery of health "in the naturall ayre of my countrey." He deplored the ill effects on the Virginia project of his return home, but argued that it would have been far worse for Virginia had he remained there only to die.

A nice advertisement this for the healthfulness of Virginia's climate. One might wonder at the council's decision to publish the report were it not for the obvious fact that the alternative would have been worse still. Some explanation had to be given the public, for the adventurers had counted heavily on the presence of Lord De la Warr in Virginia to offset the discouragement of earlier reports from Jamestown, as their promotional literature amply demonstrates. He was a nobleman, the head of a great family, and a member of His Majesty's Council for Virginia. "Now know yee," reads the commission he had received in February 1610, "that we his Majesties said Councell upon good advise and deliberation and upon notice had of the wisedome, valour, circumspection, and of the virtue and especiall sufficiencie of the Right Honourable Sir Thomas West, Knight Lord la Warr to be in principall place of authoritie and government in the said collonie, and finding in him the said Lord la Warr propensness and willingness to further and advance the good of the said plantation, by virtue of the said authoritie unto us given by the said letters pattents have nominated, made, ordained and apointed . . . the said Sir Thomas West, Knight Lord la Warr to be principall Governor, Commander and Captain Generall both by land and sea over the said colonie and all other collonies planted or to be planted in Virginia or within the limits specified in his Majesties said letters pattents and over all persons, Admiralls Vice-Admirals and other officers and commanders whether by sea or land of what qualitie soever for and during the term of his natural life, and do hereby ordaine and declare that he the said Lord la Warr during his life shall be stiled and called by the name and title of Lord Governor and Captain General of Virginia." And now, after little more than a year and before the subscribers to the new joint-stock fund had paid in their second installment, the Lord Governor and Captain General of Virginia was back in London to make a public confession that in Virginia he had nearly died of the ague, flux, and scurvy. From time to time thereafter the company publicly suggested that the Lord Governor might soon return to his post, but he did not undertake to do so until 1618 and then he died on the way.

Once more the leaders of the company showed determination. Delinquent subscribers were carried to court in a series of chancery actions extending into 1614. How much was collected in this way cannot be said, but the complaints entered in chancery have provided most helpful clues to an understanding of the company's financial history. It seems unlikely that anything collected as a result of these actions served to do more than reduce an indebtedness incurred by the company in 1611 on the promise of its subscribers. One thing is certain: there was no chance of floating another subscription. By 1612 the adventurers were complaining that only the name of God was more frequently profaned in the streets and market places of London than was the name of

Virginia. After that year the Virginia lottery, its winning tickets entitling the holder to an exchange for shares in the Virginia joint-stock, became the company's chief dependence. Now and again there would also be found some person who wanted to go to Virginia at his own cost, and was willing to pay the cost in return for shares of stock guaranteeing an ultimate title to land in the colony. These transactions, at a time when Virginia's name had lost its magic, were perhaps too few to suggest to any one of the adventurers that here was the future, not only of the company, but of English colonization in North America. Although the Virginia Company continued to be active for thirteen years after 1611, the last of its great joint-stock funds was the one to which men made their subscriptions just before Lord De la Warr came home.

To this statement perhaps a qualification should be added. Virginia at first had been to Englishmen America itself, and so it had remained in a very real sense, despite an obvious tendency since 1609 for the adventurers to pin their hopes increasingly on what might be found within the reach of Jamestown. The continuance of the Virginia adventure became thus not simply a matter of keeping the Jamestown colony alive. What mattered was that somewhere in North America the great task to which the company had committed itself should go forward. And where better, after 1611, could this be tried than in the Bermudas? Divine providence had pointed the way, so clearly that it might even be possible to raise the needed funds in London. Moreover, Sir George Somers, by being shipwrecked there and subsequently by dying there, had provided a name for the islands that was both English and suggestive of a climate so healthful that even Lord De la Warr might prosper there. Accordingly, the leading members of the Virginia Company in 1612 undertook the colonization of the Somers Islands, a designation often written as the Summer Islands, and for that purpose they subscribed to a new joint-stock fund. The Bermuda joint-stock, however, seems to have been a much more modest fund than that subscribed either in 1609 or 1611.

There was nothing unusual in thus creating within the framework of the Virginia Company a special stock for investment under the direction of its own officers and committees in the colonization of Bermuda. In the great companies of London it was customary that each stock should be separately administered. The only technical difficulty lay in the fact that Bermuda was located outside the geographical limits granted the Virginia adventurers. Under the second of their charters, rights at sea (on both seas) had extended out from the coasts for only 100 miles, which for the purposes of 1612 was not far enough. The adventurers, therefore, sought and secured a third charter granting them rights along the coast of Virginia, within the limits of 41° and 30° of northerly latitude, to a distance of 300 leagues, in order to include "divers Islands lying desolate and uninhabited, some of which are already made known and discovered by the industry, travel, and expences of the said Company, . . . all and every of which it may import the said Colony [of Virginia] both in safety and policy of trade to populate and plant."

This extension of bounds undoubtedly represents the chief reason for seeking the third Virginia charter, but the leaders of the company, while they had the opportunity, also included other significant provisions. Especially significant was a decision to enlarge the authority belonging to the general assembly of the adventurers. To its former prerogatives, which had been chiefly to elect members of the council and to determine the apportionment of lands, the third charter added three fundamental rights: to elect all officers of either company or colony, to admit new members to the fellowship of the company, and to draft laws and ordinances for the welfare of the plantation. Heretofore, the council had been the true governing body, though subject to a right of election and displacement by the adventurers in gen-

Merchants of Virginia.

THe Company of Merchants, called *Merchants of Virginia*, *Bermudas*, or *Summer-Ilands*, for (as I heare) all thefe additions are given them. I know not the time of their incorporating, neither by whom their Armes, Supporters, and Creſt were granted, and therefore am compelled to leaue them abruptly.

From John Stow, *Survey of London*, 1632

Photo by Virginia State Library.

Virginia Seal

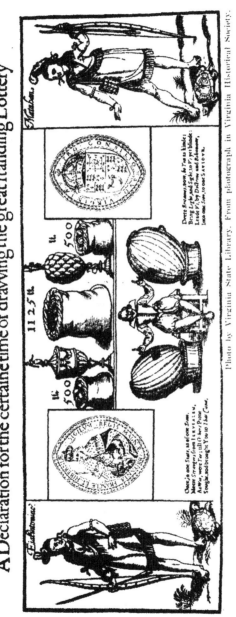

A Declaration for the certaine time of drawing the great standing Lottery

Photo by Virginia State Library. From photograph in Virginia Historical Society.

Heading for the Broadside issued by *The Virginia Company*, London, 1615

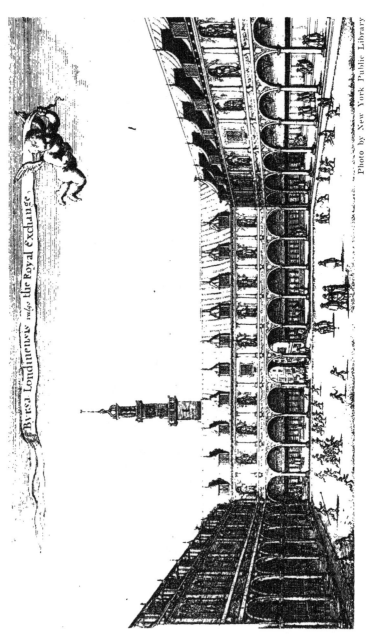

Royal Exchange, London. As it was in the time of the Virginia Company.

Captain John Smith

From *The London Company of Virginia* (New York and London, 1908)

Photo by Virginia State Library

THOMAS WEST, *Third Lord de la Warr*

From Alexander W. Weddell, *Virginia Historical Portraiture*

Photo by Virginia State Library.

SIR THOMAS SMITH (or SMYTHE)
"The Right Worſhipful Sir Thomas Smith, of London, Knight, one of his Maieſties Councell
for Virginia, and Treaſurer for the Colonie, and Gouernour of the Companies of
the Moſcovia and Eaſt India Merchants."
From the Original Portrait by an Unknown Artist, now in the poſſeſſion
of The Skinners' Company, London.

From Alexander W. Weddell, *Virginia Historical Portraiture*

Photo by Virginia State Library.

Henry Wrothesley
(Third Earl of Southampton)
from the painting by Michiel Jansz van Mierevelt

From *The London Company of Virginia* (New York and London, 1908)

SIR EDWIN SANDYS
From the Original Portrait by an Unknown Artist, now in the possession
of Sir Edmund Arthur Lechmere, Bart, Bramham Gardens,
London, England

From Alexander W. Weddell, *Virginia Historical Portraiture*

Photo by Virginia State Library.

Sir Thomas Dale

Portrait by an unknown artist of the Anglo-Flemish
School painted in oils early in the 17th Century. The
original portrait is preserved in the Virginia Museum
of Fine Arts, Richmond, Virginia

HENRY STUART
Prince of Wales

From Alexander Brown, *The Genesis of the United States*
Photo by Virginia State Library.

eral assembly. Now the general court of the adventurers was to govern, with the council as its executive agency. Since voting in the Virginia courts, as in those of other companies at the time, was by head rather than by share, this provision of the charter can be interpreted only as an attempt by the great men of the company to encourage a renewed interest on the part of the general body of adventurers by enlarging their influence on the conduct of the company's affairs. It was the third charter which also authorized the establishment of the Virginia lottery—the first of many attempts in American history to exploit the gambler's instinct for the support of a worthy cause. In the charter the king also gave assurance that his courts would view favorably the company's suits against delinquent subscribers.

The new charter having received the final seal in March 1612, a new colony was established in Bermuda in the following July. Its early history has a double significance for the later history of Virginia. In the first place, the Bermuda colony emphasizes the growing interest of the adventurers in what might be produced in America as against what might be found by way of America. The occupation of the Bermuda Islands might almost be described as a retreat from the earlier search for a passage to China. The move could be viewed also as a reassertion of an old interest in plundering the Spaniard, for the Bermudas lay athwart the homeward route of Spain's treasure fleets. But in any case the primary interest was in America and its own peculiar opportunities, and the attention given by the early settlers in Bermuda to experiments with tobacco, sugar, wine, ginger, and other such commodities suggests that their purpose was not so much to plunder the Spaniard as rather to emulate his success as a planter in the West Indies. Secondly, the adventurers showed a marked inclination to encourage each adventurer to meet his own costs. Provision was made for an early survey and division of the land, with the result that men put their money chiefly into the development of their own estates. A final survey was not completed until 1617, but at that date some of the Bermuda adventurers at least had known who their tenants were and approximately where their land would lie for three full years. Whether for these or for other reasons, Bermuda grew while Virginia languished. By 1616 over 600 colonists had reached the Somers Islands, where most of them survived. In contrast, Virginia had that year 350 people.

The Bermuda subscribers had been separately incorporated as the Somers Island Company with its own royal charter in 1615. Indeed, ever since 1612, when the Bermuda adventurers helped to relieve the financial embarrassment of the Virginia Company by paying £2,000 for its newly acquired title to Bermuda, the Somers Island adventurers seem to have functioned increasingly as a separate corporation. But the membership of the two companies was much the same. It had been the more active and interested of the Virginia adventurers who subscribed to the Bermuda joint-stock in 1612, and for twelve years thereafter the active membership of the Virginia Company came so close to duplicating the membership of the Bermuda Company that the two bodies often met virtually as one. Until 1619 Sir Thomas Smith served as governor of both companies.

The growing interest of the London adventurers after 1612 in the colonization of Bermuda did not mean that Virginia was wholly neglected. Funds secured from the lottery and from suits against delinquent subscribers were enough to keep the project alive. In 1612 the adventurers even sent out a stock of silkworms for a test of silk production. Needless to say, returning ships brought back no silk; nor did they bring sugar or wine. Lumber, including the valuable black walnut, seems to have provided the chief cargo for return voyages. A shipment of tobacco, Virginia's first, in 1614 gave some ground for arguing that the agricultural experimentation to which the colonists had been committed for several years now would pay off eventually. So argued Sir Thomas Gates on his return home this same year after three years of service in the colony, but the fact that he had come back from Virginia apparently made more of an impression than did his argument. Others also came home, their contracted term of service ended, and rarely did they bring any news from Virginia which added good to its name. Instead, they talked of the severe discipline under which they had been forced to live, and made sport of the too hopeful propaganda which had first persuaded them to become adventurers in Virginia. The discipline, chiefly associated with Dale's office as marshal, made his loyal decision to remain in the colony for another two years as lieutenant governor a further contribution to the ill repute of Virginia's name.

Dale finally came home in 1616, the year in which the dividend on the 1609 joint-stock fell due. The contrast between the high hopes of 1609 and the reality of 1616 was all too painfully apparent. Six hundred men, women, and children had sailed for Virginia in the first of these years under a plan to live and work together for a seven year period. They would share, each according to his particular skill or aptitude, in the common task of planting a colony, and they would live out of a common store. By 1616, towns were to have been built, churches and houses raised, and an increasing acreage brought under cultivation. A variety of profitable crops would have been tested, and markets established for them. The original stock of cattle would have increased through care until there were enough for all. At the same time, the trade with the Indians would have been put on a profitable basis, as would have mining operations and perhaps even a trade to Cathay. Such was the general prospect to which so many adventurers had responded in 1609. To the modern student all this seems so unrealistic as to be almost unbelievable, but unless one grasps the reality of the original dream he cannot hope to comprehend the extent of a later disillusionment.

There were no funds to be divided in 1616, but the company did declare a dividend of land—not the 500 acres per share that

Alderman Johnson had suggested as a possibility in 1609 but the more modest total of 50 acres. This 50 acres, however, was designated as a first dividend. Others would follow, for an ultimate total of perhaps 200 acres per share, as the area in the colony's "actual possession" was enlarged. Plans were announced for dispatching a new governor to Virginia with instructions for completing the necessary surveys, and the adventurers were urged to seize the opportunity to gain a desirable priority in the location of their shares by contributing £12 10s. toward meeting the necessary costs. In return for this contribution, the adventurer would be entitled to an additional 50 acres. The land now to be divided was that lying along the James River, and only those adventurers who submitted to the additional levy would be entitled to share in the division, except apparently for adventurers then living in the colony. These were the old planters, as they came to be called, whose rights paralleled those of the old adventurers in England. It is evident that the adventurers were in no position to claim a monopoly as the just reward of their past sacrifices, for they also offered an immediate dividend, on terms no different from those governing the rights of the old adventurers, to any new adventurer who wished to join by paying £12 10s. per share. Such was the estate to which the Virginia Company had been reduced after ten years of effort.

To employ a term that was destined to become common at a later period of American history, the Virginia Company had become nothing more than a land company. Its one asset was the land that had been bought with the sacrifices of the first ten years, and after 1616 all of its plans depended upon the hope that it might use its power to give title to that land as an inducement for investment in the colony. In its advertisement in 1616 adventurers, both old and new, were invited to take up shares for occupancy by themselves or for development by tenants sent for the purpose. Perhaps because the first response to this appeal was disappointing, the company provided an additional inducement in 1617 by promising 50 acres per head for every person sent to the colony, the payment being due to the one who bore the cost. This was the Virginia headright, as it came to be called, which was destined to remain the chief feature of the colony's land policy through many years after the demise of the company itself. Intended at first to encourage the adventurers in England to send the labor that was necessary for the development of the land, it served thereafter as a land subsidy of the immigration on which the colony lived and grew.

By 1618 the fortunes of Virginia were taking a turn for the better. The adventurers, or some of them at least, found encouragement in continued shipments of tobacco. These shipments were small and the quality of the tobacco could not be compared with the Spanish leaf of West Indian production which was finding a growing market in London despite King James's known disapproval of the habit on which the market grew. But the quality of Virginia tobacco, for which Sir Thomas Smith seems to have found a first market in the East Indies, no doubt could be improved as the planters learned the art of its cultivation and the adventurers found for them a better weed. No doubt, too, this success with tobacco, whatever the imperfections of the current product, could be viewed as a harbinger of other successful attempts to produce commodities the Spaniard had for so long and so profitably grown in his West Indian plantations.

Further encouragement came from the willingness of the handful of planters already in Virginia to remain there, and from the decision of Ralph Hamor and Samuel Argall, both of whom had formerly served the company in the colony, to return there. Especially significant were the arrangements under which Hamor and Argall planned their return early in 1617. One of the problems that had undoubtedly discouraged the adventurers from taking up the company's offer of a land grant in 1616 was the question of the supervision that could be provided for such tenants as they might elect to put on the land. In Bermuda, the adventurers had found an answer, or rather thought they had, by dividing the land into tribes, later designated as parishes, over which a bailif would exercise an office that was partly civil and partly traditional on the landed estates of England. In Virginia, Hamor and Argall pointed the way to a solution by entering into an association with several of the adventurers in England for the development of a jointly held plantation. Thus, in January 1617, the company awarded 16 bills of adventure to Hamor and six associates for the 16 men they proposed to transport to Virginia at their own charge. The following month saw a similar transaction with Captain Argall and his associates, five adventurers who had joined with this seasoned veteran to send out a total of 24 men. Argall went also as lieutenant governor in succession to George Yeardley, who had been left as deputy by Dale on his return to England in 1616, but the cost of getting the new governor out to his post seems to have been met entirely by his own associates. The arrangement has an obvious pertinence to an understanding of Argall's unhappy experience as governor, for he was later charged with neglect of the public interest through too great concern for his own personal interests. But here the emphasis belongs to the equally obvious fact that some of the adventurers were responding to an opportunity to send out tenants who would work under the management and direction of an experienced colonist.

In 1618 George Yeardley was back in London consulting with other adventurers, including some of the leading members of the company, who were interested in forming associations for the development of "particular plantations." Late in the year he sailed for the colony as the newly designated governor of Virginia. With him he carried instructions which record for us further developments in the company's land policy. All adventurers, including delinquents who would pay up their subscription, were now promised 100 acres of land on the first dividend for each share of stock, and another 100 acres as a second dividend after the first had been occupied. Such of the ancient planters as had paid their own way to Virginia, which was to say those who had settled at their own cost before Dale's departure in 1616, were also to receive grants in like amount. The adventurers were encouraged to pool their rights for a common grant of land by the promise that their estate could be developed under their own management and would be treated as a separate administrative unit for civil and military purposes. What the company had in mind were the larger associations already formed or on the point of being formed, such as that for the settlement of Southampton Hundred, which eventually embraced a nominal area of perhaps as much as 100,000 acres and in which the associated adventurers invested a total of some £6,000. Another example is the association of Sir William Throckmorton, Sir George Yeardley, Richard Berkeley, George Thorpe, and John Smyth of North Nibley which early in 1619 received a first joint grant of 4,500 acres and which founded above Jamestown the plantation known as Berkeley Hundred. These new associations were very much the same as the association of the Virginia adventurers which in 1612 had undertaken the colonization of Bermuda. For the development of their common grant they pooled the necessary capital in their own joint-stock fund and directed its investment through their own courts, assemblies, or committees as they saw fit. For every tenant sent to the plantation, the associated adventurers were entitled to an additional headright of 50 acres. They were awarded also an additional 1,500 acres for the support of public charges in the hundred, such as those incurred for the maintenance of a church and minister.

How many of the colonists who migrated to Virginia between 1618 and 1624 went by agreement with such associations as these is difficult to say, but there can be no doubt that they were a very large part of the total. The Virginia Company, which had served theretofore as the immediate colonizing agent, was becoming more and more a supervisory body for the encouragement of individual and associated adventurers in their own colonizing efforts. For itself, the company looked forward to a continuing revenue from quitrents to be paid, at the rate of two shillings per hundred acres after a term of seven years from the original grant, by all save the ancient adventurers and the planters who had migrated before 1616 at their own costs. To this revenue from quitrents could be added the benefit to be expected from the company's control of the colony's trade.

As in 1609, there seems to be no doubt that all plans looked ultimately to the establishment of individual land titles. Where the record has survived, the associated adventurers clearly intended that their common grant would in time be divided. In the case of Berkeley Hundred, the evidence suggests too that the associates used the promise of a share in this division for the recruitment of their first tenants. Yeardley's instructions reaffirmed the company's promise of a headright in terms inviting the migration of individual settlers at their own cost.

To understand the plans of 1618, the modern American needs to dismiss any idea that the isolated farm house of later America represented the ideal toward which men looked at this time. He should think rather of the English village community, or of the New England town, where men lived together with the advantages of a close social relationship and where the land they cultivated lay close at hand to the village and its church. If the associated adventurers continued to depend for a time on variations of the original joint-stock plan, it was not merely because they wanted to share the risk of a still uncertain venture or because they were seeking some useful device for meeting the problems of management. It was also because the plantation they hoped to establish was to have at its heart a town, and it was thought that the town could best be built through some common effort.

What has been said above is not intended to suggest that the company's role after 1618 was to be purely supervisory. Although

36

it had an accumulated debt of some £9,000, or possibly because of this debt, the company agreed for the encouragement of individual adventurers to assume heavy responsibilities of leadership. It directed Yeardley to lay out four towns, or boroughs, along the James in which grants to individuals or the lesser associations would fall—Kecoughtan at the mouth of the James, Henrico at the head of its navigation, and in between Charles City and James City. From the Bermuda adventurers the company borrowed the idea of establishing a public estate intended to meet as nearly as possible all costs of government. In each borough 3,000 acres were to be set aside as the company's land for cultivation by its own tenants, who would work at half shares. Out of the company's moiety would come the support of all superior officers, excepting the governor, for whom an additional 3,000 acres would be set aside in James City. The company thus committed itself to a not inconsiderable program of colonization on its own responsibility.

One wonders what it was that inspired this renewed, and most ambitious, venture in Virginia—a venture that would carry to Virginia over the next five years something like 4,500 colonists. Several possibilities can be suggested. First of all, it should be noted that the interest of the London adventurers in the colonization of America had never faltered, despite repeated disappointment, since they had originally laid their hands to the task in 1606. This, at any rate, is true of the adventurers who led, and more especially of Sir Thomas Smith. After it had become no longer possible to push the adventure in Virginia, they had turned to Bermuda, where an initial success seems to have encouraged another try in Virginia. The plans adopted for Bermuda and later for Virginia indicate that the adventurers shrewdly capitalized on the desire of Englishmen in many different walks of life for title to the undeveloped lands of America. A newly stirring missionary impulse had its part to play, if only by giving to the name of Virginia more helpful associations. Argall had captured

Pocahontas, the favored daughter of Powhatan, and with her as hostage the colonists had forced a peace with a heretofore implacable foe. More than that John Rolfe had married the Princess Pocahontas, as the English liked to call her, and Sir Thomas Dale as his last major service to the colony had brought her to England in 1616. In London, at court, and elsewhere, she and her entourage of Indian maidens had been a most effective advertisement of Virginia. Even after her own death in 1617, her maiden consorts had stayed on for many months before being finally returned to Virginia by way of Bermuda. Since 1613 the Virginia Company had leaned heavily on the missionary appeal in its efforts to encourage continued support of the colony, and it may well have been the company itself which prompted the bishops of the Church of England in the year of Pocahontas' death to sponsor a collection of funds for an Indian mission in Virginia. In any case, the approximately £1,500 raised for the purpose were turned over to the company, which in 1618 ordered Yeardley to set aside 10,000 acres at Henrico for the support of an Indian college.

The adventurers in 1618 also decreed certain legal and political reforms that were helpful in giving Virginia a better name than it had enjoyed for several years past. Disgruntled colonists returning from Jamestown had brought exaggerated stories of Dale's discipline, with the result that Virginia had gained the reputation almost of a penal colony. The company's renewed guarantee that the settlers would enjoy the full common law rights of Englishmen at home was coupled with provision for a general assembly of the colonists, a body which first met at Jamestown in 1619. In short, the company had the benefit in 1618, as so frequently in the past, of leadership of the highest quality.

Sir Thomas Smith was still the governor of the company in 1618, and without question his leadership must be considered to be a major factor shaping the new life then being infused into the colony. But a factional strife that would soon help to destroy the company already had made its appearance. The sources of this factionalism were varied, and some of them had little to do with the affairs of Virginia. Thus, at this time Sir Thomas found a determined enemy in the Rich family, headed by the wealthy Earl of Warwick and represented most ably by Sir Nathaniel Rich, who for many years was an active leader in the House of Commons. Warwick had a way of investing in voyages which bordered closely on piracy, and as a result of one such investment had become involved in a long and bitter conflict with Smith as the governor of the East India Company. Unquestionably of more fundamental importance was a growing opposition to Smith that was based upon discontent with the former management of the Virginia project. It seems almost as though the Virginia adventurers, before they could place full confidence in the new program for the colony's development, had to find some more satisfying explanation for the company's previous failures by charging gross mismanagement of its affairs. Such, at any rate, was the conviction to which many adventurers came, chiefly it would seem the lesser adventurers who were easily prejudiced against the great merchants of London, of whom Sir Thomas was the chief. In a company where the ultimate power to decide had been vested since 1612 in a general assembly of the adventurers voting by head rather than by share, the discontent of the lesser adventurers could become under the guidance of an effective leader a very potent force.

The leader was found in Sir Edwin Sandys, one of the ablest parliamentarians of seventeenth century England. Sandys himself was not one of the lesser adventurers. He had been a member of the Virginia Council since 1607, and in 1611 he had responded to the company's appeal for a subscription of £37 10s. by subscribing double that amount, thereby matching the subscription of Sir Thomas Smith. With the aid of other prominent adventurers, including the Earl of Southampton, and by making common cause for the moment with the Rich faction, Sir Edwin won election to the governorship of the company in the spring of 1619. In the absence of anything approaching a full record, it is impossible to say what justification there may have been for the charges of mismanagement that were brought against Smith's administration. It would not be surprising if over the long and frequently discouraging years of his leadership, and especially in the period since 1612, some irregularities, some carelessness had crept into the conduct of the company's business. A very noticeable result of Sandys' election was an effort to systematize the company's procedures by adoption of new standing orders and regulations, and to bring order out of an alleged confusion of the company's records, especially those pertaining to the rights of the adventurers to land in Virginia. But it is possible to speak with full assurance on only one point: no other of the adventurers had shown more courage or more devotion to the colony, no other of them deserves to be better remembered than Sir Thomas Smith.

There can be no question, however, that the reviving interest in Virginia received an additional stimulant from the fact that the business now had a new management. At the close of 1618, and largely as the result of emigration during that year, the population of the colony stood at approximately 1,000 persons. During the year after Sandys' election, a total of 1,261 emigrants left England for Virginia, over 800 of them at the company's charge. This substantial evidence of the company's determination to assume the lead encouraged additional associations of adventurers to take up patents for their own plantations, with the result that by the summer of 1622 the council could announce that over 3,500 people had migrated to Virginia since the spring of 1619. This was a remarkable record, testifying to the very great gifts Sir Edwin possessed as a leader and the confidence men placed in his leadership.

The minutes of the company's courts have survived for the period after the election of Sandys, and so it is possible to get a clearer picture of the company's organization and procedures than can be had for any earlier date. Further help comes from the "Orders and Constitutions" drawn up after Sandys' election and published in 1620 as part of a pamphlet skilfully written to convey the impression that Virginia's affairs were then being managed much better than in the past. The company depended basically upon decisions reached in four great quarter courts, which were general assemblies of all the adventurers who wished to attend and which were scheduled for regular meeting on next to the last Wednesday of each of the quarterly terms in which the king's courts sat at Westminster. Only a quarter court could elect officers, either of the colony or of the company, enact laws and ordinances, or determine policies governing the distribution of lands in the colony and the conduct of its trade. On the Monday preceding each meeting of the quarter court, a preparatory court would settle the agenda for the following Wednesday, in order that the members might have warning of the business to be taken up at that time. Each fortnight, except in the "long vacations" between court terms, an ordinary court would meet, again on Wednesday, with a quorum that required the presence of at least five members of the council, the treasurer or his deputy, and "fifteene of the generality." The hour of meeting for all courts was 2 P.M., and at no court could a question be put after 6 P.M. A decision reached by any lesser court, including the extraordinary court that might be called in case of special emergency, could be overridden by a quarter court. This was the governing body of the company, a popular assembly in which Sir Edwin often demonstrated his special talent as a parliamentary tactician. Attendance varied according to the importance of the business at hand, but as many as 150 might attend.

The quarter court meeting in Easter term was a court of elections, where the members cast their votes for all principal officers by secret ballot. Except for members of the council, all offices of the company were held by annual election. The chief office was that of the treasurer, as the governor of the company was still officially designated. As frequently as not, in common usage he was known as the governor, but the charters had fixed the title of his office and in so doing had pointed up a primary responsibility of the office. The governor of the Virginia Company was in fact its treasurer. After 1619 no man could hold the position for longer than three years, and no man was eligible for election to it if already he was serving as the governor of another company, except that he might also serve as the governor of the Somers Island Company. The election court might vote a reward for services rendered, but the treasurer, like other principal officers, served without fixed compensation.

His chief assistant, and the second officer in rank, was the deputy. As the title suggests, he might be deputized to perform virtually any function of the governor, including that of presiding at courts in the governor's absence. But he also had important functions of his own. He is perhaps best described as the chief administrative officer of the company. He was specifically charged with superintendence over all lesser officers, and he had a primary responsibility for contracts and other business arrangements relating to the dispatch of shipping, provisions, and passengers to Virginia and to the receipt, storage, and marketing of cargoes returned from the colony. At all times, he acted, or was supposed to act, in accordance with instructions from the court, council, or treasurer, but all such instructions were necessarily general in character. Many were the opportunities to use his own judgment, or to confer a favor, as he handled business transactions involving hundreds or even thousands of pounds. For his assistance and perhaps to keep a watch on him, he had a committee of sixteen men chosen by the court under a provision requiring that a fourth of the number should be changed each year "to the end [that] many be trained up in the businesse." The committee may have been new, but the deputy's office was old. It had been occupied for many years before the spring election of 1619 by Alderman Johnson. Some of the more serious charges brought against Smith's administration related to the management of the magazine, as the stock of supplies periodically forwarded to the colony was generally described. Johnson had managed the successive magazines, each separately financed by its own joint-stock, until in 1619 he was replaced by John Ferrar.

The council, still described as His Majesty's Council for Virginia, had become a large and unwieldy body, with many of its members inactive. Its influence on the conduct of Virginia's affairs was now decidedly less important than in the earlier years. According to the Orders and Constitutions, no one "under the degree of a Lord or principall magistrate" was thereafter to be elected to the council except "such as by diligent attendance at the courts and service of Virginia for one year at least before, have approved their sufficiency and worth to the Companie." As this statement strongly suggests, a place on the council was for many members an honorary post through which one might lend the prestige of a great name to a worthy undertaking without assuming much real responsibility. Nevertheless, the legal powers of the council under the Virginia charters made its services indispensable, and made it desirable that at least a few of its members should be intimately acquainted with the business. The treasurer was supposed to consult with the council on important occasions, and especially on matters pertaining to the government of the colony. All formal instructions to officers in the colony had to be sent in the name of the council and over its seal. In any case of removal from office, in London or at Jamestown, the cause had to be considered in council before it could be taken before the adventurers. But any seven members made a quorum giving full power to actions taken in council, and the treasurer, who was always a member of the council, had the custody of its seal.

Two of the seven auditors now required for annual review of disbursements and receipts had to be members of the council. The auditors' office had grown out of the disputes over the accounts of Sir Thomas Smith, and in addition to the annual audit-

43

ing of the treasurer's report, which had to be submitted to the Easter court, they were charged with responsibility for a close review of all earlier records of the company. The primary purpose was to establish a full and exact list of all subscriptions, with notation especially of delinquencies. Salaried officers of the company were a secretary, a bookkeeper, a husband (or as we would say, an accountant), and a bedel or messenger. The secretary served all courts held by the adventurers, the council, and the auditors, or by standing and special committees, of which last the adventurers appointed quite a number. In addition, the secretary was custodian of the company's records.

Although Sir Edwin Sandys continued to be the actual leader of the company until its dissolution in 1624, his tenure of the treasurer's office was limited to a single year. When the adventurers assembled for the annual elections in the spring of 1620, they were much disturbed to receive instruction from the king that Sir Edwin was not to be re-elected. Instead, the king suggested the choice of some merchant of means and wide experience—perhaps Sir Thomas Smith, Sir Thomas Roe, Alderman Robert Johnson, or Mr. Maurice Abbott.

Whether Sandys could have been elected in the absence of this interference by the king, which the adventurers protested as an unwarranted invasion of their liberty, is itself an interesting and debatable question. By his many criticisms of the previous conduct of the company's affairs, Sandys had won the undying enmity of Sir Thomas Smith and his important friends. More than that, he had quarreled with his ally of the preceding year, the Earl of Warwick, who had connections hardly less impressive than those enjoyed by Sir Thomas. The quarrel with Warwick was over a question of piracy, as Sir Edwin chose to regard it. One of Warwick's ships, the *Treasurer*, had sailed from England in April 1618 with a license to capture pirates, which was one way of getting a ship cleared from English ports for depredations against the Spaniard at a time when the king had set his face against all such activity. The *Treasurer* had called at Jamestown, where Governor Argall, who had rendered important services to the colony but who had special reason to understand that his position in Virginia depended upon the good will of important members of the company, helped to outfit the vessel for a raid on the West Indies. Recent studies, and especially those of David Quinn, a British scholar, argue strongly that the earlier ventures of Gilbert and Raleigh had been inspired very largely by the desire to establish some base on the North American coast that would be useful in attacks upon Spanish possessions and the trade routes which joined them to Spain. But it is evident enough that by this time the leaders of the Virginia Company were chiefly fearful that Spain might attack their colony before it was securely fortified, and before it had fulfilled the promise of rewards far greater than anything freebooting ventures could offer. As a result, Governor Yeardley, on instruction from London, denied the courtesies of Jamestown to the *Treasurer* on its return in 1619, and won for Sandys thereby the bitter resentment of the Rich family.

The king's interference in the election of 1620 has naturally become a celebrated incident in the history of Virginia. Sir Edwin was a leader in parliament, which before the century was out would establish its supremacy in the government of England, and the Virginia Company in 1620 had only recently established the first representative assembly in North America. To historians who have sought the larger meaning of the American experiment, it has often seemed that the king must have been guided by a fear of representative government—in other words, that his motives were largely political. No doubt, he was more easily persuaded to enter an objection to Sandys' re-election because of Sir Edwin's opposition to royal policies in the house of commons, but there is no contemporary evidence to suggest that the king had even noticed the Assembly which met at Jamestown in 1619. Moreover, that Assembly had been authorized before Sandys' election, at a time when Sir Thomas Smith was still in the chair, and anyone who thinks the motion had been carried over Smith's opposition should take note that the same kind of representative assembly was established in 1620 for Bermuda, over whose fortunes Sir Thomas would continue to preside until 1621. Not until the middle of the seventeenth century, at the time of Cromwell, does it appear that anyone even suggested that the primary reason for the king's interference was fear of a significant development in the history of representative government.

What actually happened in 1620 would seem to be clear enough. Sir Thomas Smith had connections that reached all the way into the king's bedchamber, and there he effectively argued that Sandys did not know his business. It was an argument that found not a little justification in the fact that the company had to admit by a broadside published in the very month of the election court that hundreds of the colonists sent to Virginia in the preceding year had died within a short time of their arrival there, and it may be that Sir Thomas apprehended the even greater disasters soon to overtake the colony. A more likely supposition, however, is that he seized upon this news from the colony as an opportunity to vent his resentment against Sandys, a resentment that must have become more bitter with each of Sir Edwin's promotional releases advertising the great improvements now to be found in the management of Virginia's affairs. The legal basis on which the king acted was probably debatable. No doubt, he depended upon the provision in the charter requiring that all members of the council, of which the treasurer was the head, be sworn to the king's service. But membership on the council was for life, and Sir Edwin had taken his oath as a member of the council as early as 1607. Perhaps the king took advantage of the company's regulations requiring an annual election and that the treasurer be sworn following his election. Whether this was a new requirement cannot be said. It can only be suggested that the king intended to say that if Sir Edwin were re-elected he would not give him a necessary oath of office. It may be, too, that he stood quite simply on the prerogative of his office to insist that his subjects in Virginia were entitled to royal protection. In any case, the adventurers chose not to defy the king's wish.

Having protested his interference as unwarranted, the quarter court in May 1620 adjourned without electing a treasurer. Instead, the adventurers appointed a special committee to call on the king for the purpose of acquainting him with the true facts regarding "the managing of their business this last year" and to ask for a free election. Sandys himself appealed to the royal favorite, the young Duke of Buckingham, but with no effect on the king's decision. When the adventurers reassembled late in June, they elected the Earl of Southampton as treasurer. Thus, in a sense both parties to the dispute emerged victorious. Sandys was no longer treasurer, but the adventurers had refused to elect a merchant and Southampton would preside thereafter in behalf of Sandys. There can be no doubt that Sandys continued to be the leader of the company. Moreover, in 1621 he extended his power by gaining control of the Somers Island Company through the election of Southampton to its governorship.

A question that naturally arises is that of how, or why, Sir Edwin was able to survive this challenge to his leadership. The news from Virginia was by no means encouraging. Given the long record of disappointment there, and the many men who previously had died there, the fact that several hundred of the most recent settlers had succumbed might have been expected to unsettle any administration. Perhaps it was the king's interference, serving as it did to rally the adventurers in defence of the company's liberty. Perhaps Sir Thomas was guilty of too naked a display of his power, with the result that the lesser adventurers, who already had been taught to view the great merchants of the company with suspicion, rallied to the support of

Sandys. Perhaps it was because the Earl of Warwick and Sir Thomas had not learned yet the need for effective teamwork; both men disliked Sandys, but they had their own quarrels and they would not form a real coalition against him for another two years. All these possibilities must be given consideration, but there would seem to be still another reason, possibly the most important of all.

Sir Edwin Sandys was a man of remarkable gifts, and nowhere are these gifts better demonstrated than in his ability to stimulate the highest hopes for Virginia. Before him only Richard Hakluyt, a patriot now dead four years, had managed better to depict the promise America held for Englishmen. Sandys wrote no major work on the subject, and even the company's promotional pamphlets, which he undoubtedly shaped in some large part, lacked the fire that Hakluyt, or even Alderman Johnson, could impart to that branch of literature. It must be said also that Sandys added no new idea to those which for a generation past had guided Englishmen in their American ventures. His program included not a single objective that the Virginia Company had not theretofore tried to realize; the chief contrast with former programs was the absence of any emphasis on the prospect that a route to the South Seas might be found, an objective the adventurers had dropped for all practical purposes a good many years before Sandys became their treasurer. But Sandys had confidence, a systematic and orderly mind, and a persuasive way of talking in the quarter court or in conference with the individual adventurer who contemplated some new risk of capital. As a result, he managed to convey the impression that plans had now been so well thought through that Hakluyt's objectives in America had at last become attainable.

Leaving aside the search for a passage to China, which may never have been so important to Hakluyt as it was to the people whose interest in America he sought to enlist, Sandys undertook to carry through, all at once, the program Hakluyt had outlined for Queen Elizabeth as early as 1584 in his famous *"Discourse on Western Planting."* It was a program that looked to the development in America of products that would free England of dependence upon trades with other parts of the world which were in any way disadvantageous to England, and that would guarantee to any Englishmen who developed such products a sure profit on their investment. It was a program that had taken its shape first from the prospect, in Raleigh's day, of an early war with Spain, and perhaps it should be noted that when Sandys came to office in 1619 the Thirty Years War had only recently had its beginning with the king's own son-in-law a central figure. The war has gone down in our history books as the last of the great religious wars, and many were the Englishmen who thought that England should be, or would be soon involved.

In Virginia, Sandys promised to produce iron. It is strange that the attempt to develop an iron industry in Virginia, on which the company spent all told something like £5,000, should have made less impression on modern historians than has an early and brief search for gold that was incidental to other explorations. The iron industry in England was suffering from the depletion of the island's wood supply, which was still depended upon for smelting, and Virginia promised an unlimited supply. Other industries that he hoped to develop in the colony are suggested by a list of tradesmen the company invited to adventure to Virginia in 1620: among them, sawyers, joiners, shipwrights, millwrights, coopers, weavers, tanners, potters, fishermen, fishhookmakers, netmakers, leather dressers, limeburners, and dressers of hemp and flax. Even more important because so much depended upon persuading the individual adventurers to invest their own money in the development of their land, were plans for the production of sugar, wine, indigo, silk, cotton, olive oil, rice, etc. In the development of these products Sandys intended the public lands—those cultivated under the direct supervision of the company and by its own tenants—to serve more or less in the capacity of experimental farms. For their planting he sought seeds and plants from various parts of the world. On the college land he had some 10,000 grapevines set out, and sent for their care foreign experts imported from the continent. To make sure that private estates would not be devoted wholly to tobacco, as yet the colony's only proven staple, he wrote into land patents a stipulation that other staples would be given a trial.

To find the money for investment in the public lands was no easy task. No common joint-stock fund could be raised in 1619, if only because the company's plans depended chiefly upon the hope of inducing the adventurers to invest in their own lands. It cannot be said how successful were the renewed attempts to collect from delinquent subscribers, but perhaps some help came from that source. Sandys depended also, as had Smith before him, on the Virginia lottery, perhaps more than upon any other source, for the lottery was terminated early in 1621 by order of the privy council on grounds that included the complaint of parliament that the lottery had become a public nuisance. A very substantial help to Sir Edwin was the bishops' fund for an Indian college and additional funds raised for the support of an Indian school in the colony. The total ran to better than £2,000. It had been decided in 1618, well before Sandys' election, that the money from the bishops' fund would be invested in an estate to be known as the College Land, and the precedent thus set was followed in disposing of funds subsequently made available to the company for an Indian school. In practical terms, these decisions meant that all mission funds were used to send out tenants on the promise that a half-share of the wine and other such commodities as they might produce would in time provide a permanent endowment for the school and the college. The decision reflects both the extraordinary poverty of the company and the extraordinary confidence with which its leaders approached their new ventures in Virginia.

By the spring of 1621, when the bulk of the college funds had

50

been expended and the lottery was terminated, Sir Edwin's financial resources had become even more skimpy and uncertain. Some projects, such as that for the settlement of Italian glass-workers who were to manufacture pottery and beads for use in the Indian trade, could be financed by subscriptions to a special joint-stock, but this device offered no help in meeting general expenses. As a result, Sandys continued to take certain shortcuts, or perhaps the blame should rest rather on Deputy John Ferrar. In any case, the colonists complained that shipping came out so overloaded with passengers as to invite the epidemic disease with which they usually suffered on landing, and which made of newcomers a useless burden on the colony for some time after their arrival. The deathrate among the colonists continued to be high. The time and energy required to house them, or to feed them, unavoidably forced delay with projects on which Sandys had pinned his chief hopes. He was especially disappointed over the slow progress of agricultural experimentation. Accordingly, when Yeardley's three year term was ended in 1621 and Sir Francis Wyatt was sent as his replacement, Sir Edwin also sent his brother, George Sandys, as appointee to a new office of treasurer. He was given special charge of all projects looking to the development of new staple commodities and was intrusted with the collection of rents, of which the company claimed £1,000 were presently due. These rents, which were to be collected largely from half-share tenants who had migrated within the preceding three years, undoubtedly now constituted the company's main hope for an immediate revenue. Except in a very few instances, no quitrents would be payable until 1625, and so general had been the disappointment experienced so far with special projects that further time would have to be allowed before any return from them could be expected. In short, the company had exhausted its very limited resources in getting Wyatt and George Sandys out to Virginia, and had nothing left but hopes for the future and the anticipation of a small immediate revenue from the rents of its own tenants, most of which had already been assigned to such special charges as the support of public officers in the colony. In London, virtually the only asset left to the company was the will and determination of Sir Edwin Sandys.

In these circumstances, Sandys necessarily devoted his main energies after 1621 to the problem of tobacco, the only marketable staple the colony had as yet produced. It was an old problem, but one now filled with new difficulties. In earlier days, when it had been hoped that tobacco might be one of a variety of staples produced in the colony, the Virginia Company, like the Bermuda Company, had lent encouragement to efforts looking to its production. But hardly had early experiments proved successful before the adventurers faced the risk that tobacco would take over the colony entirely. There is nothing surprising in this development, for a tobacco plant, unlike a grapevine or an olive tree, matures within a few months of its planting, and the tobacco habit at this time was a thing of comparably rapid growth in many parts of the world. To settlers who had been staked by adventurers ever insistent upon a prompt return of their capital, or who wondered how best to procure the means to make payment for the supplies brought in the next magazine ship, the obvious answer was to plant the land to tobacco. After doing this, if time and energy remained, they might try some of Sir Edwin Sandys' ideas—maybe set out a few grapevines or mulberries, as they had been instructed to do. There was good reason for the growing fear among the leading adventurers in London that tobacco might put a blight on all other projects.

More than that, the increasing shipments of tobacco, especially in view of the still relatively poor quality of the Virginia leaf, gave the colony a bad name just when its good name was so important to the promotional efforts of the company. The tobacco habit did not yet have the respectable associations it would later acquire in the eighteenth century. Instead, it was associated with tippling or bawdy houses, where in truth a pipe was most easily had by the contemporary resident of London. Moral considerations were reinforced by an additional concern for the public interest. So much of the weed consumed came from Spain that thoughtful men were inclined to consider how much England paid out, to the profit of the Spaniard, for a commodity which added nothing to the well being of the country. Had it not been for the influence of Virginia and Bermuda adventurers in the House of Commons, Parliament in 1621 might well have prohibited all importation of tobacco into England. And in all England there was no more vigorous opponent of tobacco than the king himself. Indeed, the king had even written a book on the subject.

The attitude of King James had a most important bearing on another angle of the problem. Under its charter, the company had been allowed a seven year exemption from import duties on cargoes brought from Virginia. When this exemption expired in 1619, the government immediately imposed a duty that was fixed early in 1620 at 1s. per pound of tobacco. Though this was only half the duty paid by Spanish tobacco, it was nonetheless a heavy burden to be imposed upon leaf that was declared never to have sold at more than 5s. a pound and that brought an average of only 2s. for the better grade in 1620.* The adventurers' attempted escape by shipping their tobacco to Holland won them a sharp reprimand from the privy council, and an order to bring all of Virginia's tobacco to England for payment of his majesty's customs. As negotiations with the king's ministers for some relief continued, it was proposed in 1622 that the Virginia and Bermuda adventurers might take over the tobacco monopoly, which was a grant of the sole right to import tobacco of any sort into the kingdom in return for a fixed contribution to the royal revenues. The holder of such a monopoly—a very common device at the time—was entitled to collect the customs and to hope that what

---

*For purposes of comparison, it may be noted that Spanish tobacco was declared to have been sold for as much as 20s. a pound. The "filthy weed" was not yet "the poor man's luxury."

he collected, plus the advantage of a monopolistic control of the market, might enable him to clear a profit on the transaction. Here, in other words, was a proposal that might provide the needed relief, even some income for the company's hard pressed treasury. The Virginia Company by 1622 was in no position to ignore such an opportunity and fortunately, the Sandys faction was now in control of the Somers Island Company. A joint committee of the two companies, headed by Sir Edwin himself, entered into negotiations for what was known as the tobacco contract.

The bitterest factional strife in the history of the London adventurers soon followed. It is a complicated story, too complicated and too long to be told fully here. Briefly, both the terms agreed upon by Sandys and his proposals for the management of the contract, proposals which left Sandys and his cohorts in full control, touched too closely the vital interests of some of his bitterest enemies. In Bermuda, as in Virginia, the hope of an early profit from the production of sugar, silk, wine, indigo, and other such commodities had proved vain, and like Virginia, Bermuda lived by the tobacco it grew. The Earl of Warwick and members of his family had made especially heavy investments in their Bermuda properties, and Sir Nathaniel Rich became the floor leader, as it were, of an attempt to defeat the contract. Sir Thomas Smith and his friends joined in the effort. Especially objectionable in the view of the opposition were plans for placing the management of the contract in the hands of salaried officials, with Sir Edwin as director at a salary of £500. At one Virginia court, meeting early in December, the debate got so out of hand that it required several additional sessions to straighten out the minutes in order that appropriate penalties might be imposed upon Mr. Samuel Wrote, a member of the Virginia council whose unrestrained charges of graft violated the company's rules and offended the court's sense of its own dignity. In the end the opposition elected to make the final test in a Bermuda court, whose consent was necessary to close the contract and where Sandys' opponents included the more substantial investors in that colony. The test came in February 1623, and Sandys won. But it could be demonstrated that had the vote been by share rather than by head, as was the rule in both companies, he would have been defeated. Sandys' opponents in the Bermuda Company all along had complained of a plan to distribute the charges of the contract equally between the two companies, arguing that the Virginia tobacco had a greater value and should therefore carry a proportionately larger charge. And now they were in a position to argue that the Virginia Company, in whose courts for some time they had steadfastly refused even to vote on the salary question, sought to exploit the younger plantation, as was evidenced by the opposition of the adventurers to whom Bermuda's tobacco chiefly belonged. With this argument, Sandys' opponents promptly carried the whole question before the privy council.

This was in the spring of 1623. During the course of the preceding debate, news had come of an Indian massacre in Virginia that had cost the lives of over 350 colonists. The faction-ridden and bankrupt company had stirred itself to send such aid as it could, but now came the word that this had not been enough. By the testimony of Sandys' own brother, though this testimony may not have been immediately available to his enemies, another 500 colonists had died before the year was out as a result of the dislocations occasioned by the massacre, and as a result of the failure of the company to send enough aid. The tobacco contract dropped into a position of secondary importance as Sandys' opponents, with Alderman Johnson taking the lead, petitioned the king for a full investigation of the situation in Virginia and of the recent conduct of its affairs.

Whatever one may think of Sir Edwin Sandys, or of the motives which inspired his opponents, there can be no question as to the correctness of the action taken by the government. The leaders of the two factions were called before the privy council on April

17, where they displayed so "much heat and bitterness" toward one another as to make it difficult to get on with the business. In the end, the council won agreement that a special commission should be established for an investigation of the state of the colony's affairs, the agreement coming finally when the council conceded the demand of Sandys' supporters that the investigation should begin with the administration of Sir Thomas Smith. Accordingly, on May 9, a commission was issued to Sir William Jones, justice of the Court of Common Pleas, and six other gentlemen "to examine the carriage of the whole business." Meantime, a letter had been prepared by the privy council to acquaint the colonists with the fact that their affairs had been taken into "His Majesty's pious and princely care" and to encourage them "to go on cheerfully in the work they have in hand." The central issues all pertained to Virginia, but in the circumstances there was no choice but to include both companies in the province of the Jones commission.

The appointment of the Jones commission ended, for all practical purposes, the control of the Virginia Company over the colony. The company lingered on as an agency chiefly through which the Sandys faction prepared its briefs for the attention of the commissioners, or through which orders from the commissioners might be implemented. All of the company's records were impounded by the commission, which also took charge of all correspondence with the colony. The records of the company demonstrated all too clearly the bankrupt state of its finances. The hearings before the commissioners demonstrated with equal clarity the hopeless division of the adventurers by bitter factional strife. Correspondence from the colony brought evidence of a desperate situation. Even Sandys had to admit that no more than 2,500 colonists were still alive in the colony, which was to confess an attrition, mainly by death, of something over 40 percent of the colonists residing in Virginia, or sent to Virginia, since he had assumed responsibility for the management of its affairs. Actually, the situation was much worse than these figures suggested, for a census taken in Virginia early in 1625 showed a total population of only 1,275. In the fall of 1623 the privy council invited the company to surrender its charter on the promise that a new one would be issued to cover all individual rights and grants, but with a revision of the plan of government that would place the control of the colony under the more immediate supervision of the king. In effect, the proposal was to return to something close to the original plan of 1606. When the adventurers, in a court from which Sandys' enemies largely absented themselves, rejected this proposal, the government began quo warranto proceedings against the company in the court of Kings Bench. On May 24, 1624, that court gave its decision for recall of the Virginia charters. And so ended the Virginia Company.

The Bermuda Company had been dragged into the investigation chiefly because of the close ties joining it to the older company. There was no emergency in the colony, and its debts were not beyond the capacity of Sir Thomas Smith and other leading adventurers to pay. As a result, the Somers Island Company lasted on for another sixty years.

One who looks back from 1624 over the brief and frequently troubled history of the Virginia Company may debate, as historians have often done in the past, just what should be said by way of conclusion. Perhaps it is this: here were men who out of their disappointment quarreled bitterly and by their quarrels helped to destroy an agency through which in the past they had worked together, with a remarkable devotion to the public interest, for the achievement of great objectives. No doubt, their greatest fault had been to set their goals too high. Certainly, their greatest virtue was persistence in the faith that great things could be done for England in America, a faith destined in time to be justified by the course of history.

CPSIA information can be obtained at www.ICGtesting.com
Printed in the USA
LVOW04s0404020615

440757LV00012B/152/P